Harley Has Great Grands

Lucas Frey

ISBN 978-1-63885-155-4 (Paperback)
ISBN 978-1-63885-157-8 (Hardcover)
ISBN 978-1-63885-156-1 (Digital)

Covenant Books, Inc.
11661 Hwy 707
Murrells Inlet, SC 29576
www.covenantbooks.com

For Kay, Todd, Matt, Leigh Ann, Greg, Gordie, and Grant: my hope is reading this will bring back nothing but great memories and a lot of smiles.

For Allison and Stephanie and all great- and great-great-grandkids: I hope you can get to know the grands the way I did and teach our grandbabies these lessons. Know how much I love you all!

Harley's Grand Adventures

Riding with Grandpa GG in his old Edsel brings Harley smiles.
With the top down, the trip goes fast even though it's lots of miles.

Floating on the lake feels like time is standing still,
Especially when the sun dips down behind the hill.

Harley rides the waves, skiing in the sun.
Dolly, the boat Grandpa GG made, is always rarin' to run.

Fishing with Grandpa GG and friends makes for good times.
Harley is happy then even happier when the dinner bell chimes.

Grandpa Frey's silly dinner woofs spark laughter in us all.
Harley looks high and low but never finds the call.

Days with Grandma Frey in her vegetable garden are a delight.
Harley works and plays all day then sleeps away the night.

When summer becomes winter and snow covers the hillside,
Grandma GG uncovers the sleds and takes Harley for a ride.

I tell you these tales on the run.
Because grands are amazing and so much fun!

Harley's Grands in God's Plans

Harley's grands help people at their church,
Cooking, cleaning, and giving rides so no one's left in the lurch.

Grandpa Frey was known for building important roads.
They have paved the way for drivers and their huge loads.

He never mentions it, but Grandpa GG used to fix tanks for Allies in Europe.
At the moment, he is more worried that he ran out of maple syrup.

24

Grandpa GG volunteers at the village fire department,
Rescuing animals and putting out fires when sent.

I tell you these thoughtful tales of grands helping most.
They are so wonderful it makes me want to boast.

Grands'
Rewarding
Works

Hard work isn't always fun.
Harley has learned it must still be done.

Grandmas buy ingredients to make tasty treats.
In order to get one, Harley does amazing feats.

34

35

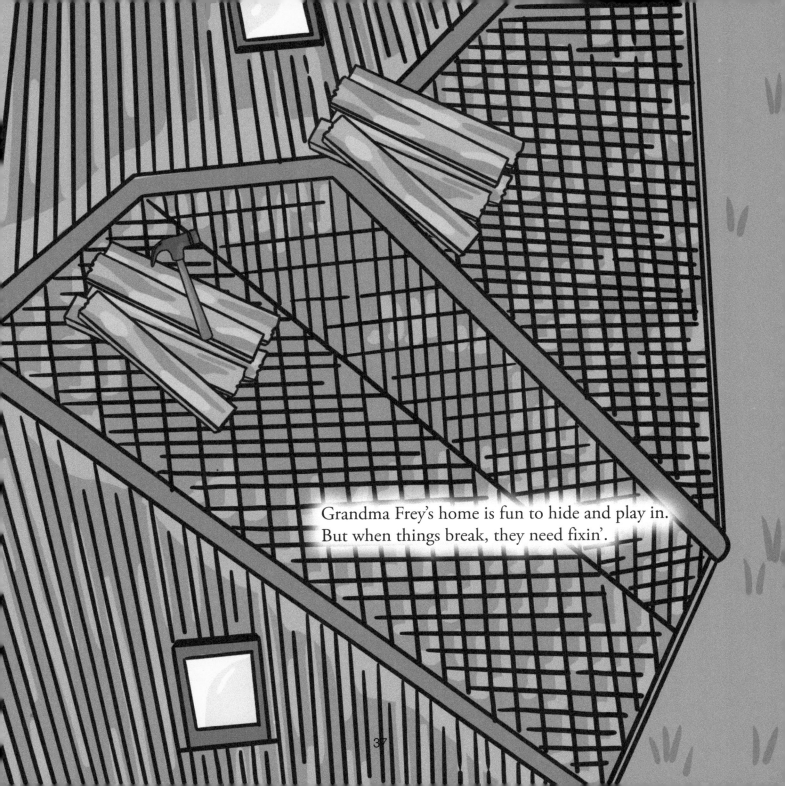

Grandma Frey's home is fun to hide and play in.
But when things break, they need fixin'.

Grandpa GG makes beautiful things with his hands,
Cutting, sanding, staining, and enjoying the time it demands.

All grands work hard in their own shops.
Harley helps and is rewarded with doggie pops.

41

Harley's grands teach her it is important to work hard,
Cleaning dishes, snow shoveling, and mowing the yard.

44

Grandma Frey's flower garden is the talk of the city.
She teaches Harley it takes hard work and love to make it so pretty.

Grandpa GG states, "If you're not ten minutes early, you're late."
This important lesson is one Harley keeps straight.

RECEPTION

I tell you these tales with good cheer.
Hard work isn't often easy, but always hold it dear.

Grands Teach
Harley Love

"Love is a many-splendored thing," grands often say.
Harley feels her grands' love every day.

When Harley was young, she ate dinner in a cast. Grandpa GG made a great chair for her, complete with a mast.

55

Harley has games all her grands attend.
They cheer her on 'til their voices reach their end.

Harley knows her grandpas aren't quick to give attention.
She knows they love her with great intention.

Grandmas make each meal with love and compassion.
Healthy food is never out of fashion.

61

When Harley is sick, her grandmas get the job done.
They feed her and love her until she can return to fun.

Sometimes the grands teach Harley hard lessons.
Things can be dangerous with her play sessions.

Kind words are what Harley hears her grands speak daily,
Words about love and happiness, spoken gayly.

I tell you this tale with a heart filled with love.
Grands are God's creations to us from above.

Grands
Teach Harley
Patience

"Life isn't always unicorns and rainbows," Harley's grands say.
Strong faith in God will light your way.

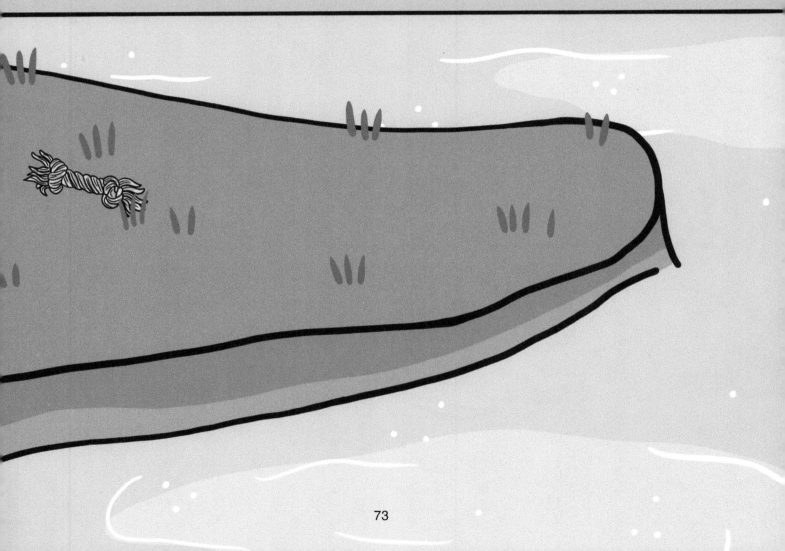

In one hundred plus years, Grandma GG has seen a lot.
The Spanish flu, wars, storms, and now covid she has not forgot.

Grandpa Frey smiles brightly each time Harley gives him a hug.
"This limp has never stopped me," he says with a shrug.

Grandma Frey makes amazing Christmas springerles to eat.
Just one smell and Harley is eager to taste the treat.

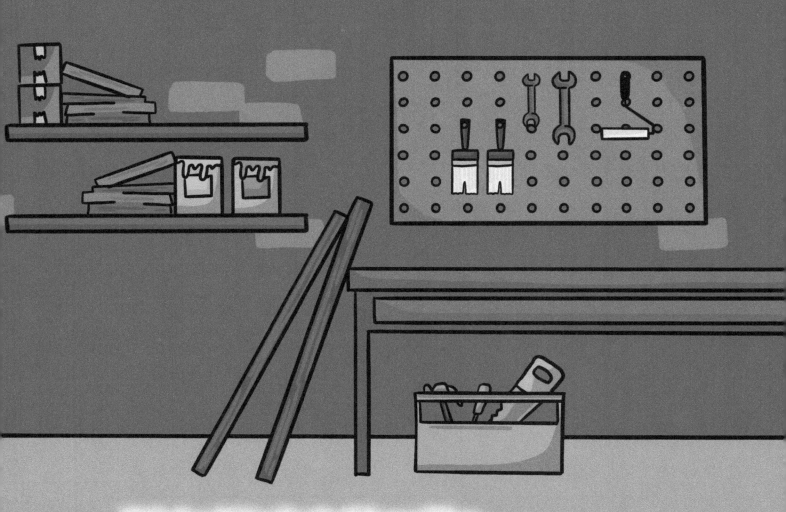

Harley loves helping Grandpa GG get stuff done.
It takes the patience of Job to teach Harley why making things is fun.

I tell you these tales about why patience pays.
Grands know the peace and serenity of its ways.

About the Author

Grandparents are incredible, and Luke has been blessed knowing, growing up, learning, and loving all four of his in a small northwest Ohio farming town called Wauseon. He graduated from Wauseon High School and the University of Cincinnati with a mechanical engineering degree. After six years as an industrial engineer (three in Honduras, Central America, with his wife and two children), Luke started a new franchise in Cincinnati and lived with his family in Terrace Park, Ohio, from 1998 until 2018. During his time in Terrace Park, Luke volunteered for the fire department and became its chief in 2007. His two beautiful daughters, Allison and Stephanie, and his wife, Connie, along with all family members, are his world.

CPSIA information can be obtained
at www.ICGtesting.com
Printed in the USA
BVHW021358210222
629674BV00017B/586